MASTERING PRODUCTIVITY FOR SMALL BUSINESS OWNERS

Tools and Techniques for Efficiency

DAVID M ARNOLD
CRYSTAL COAST HR

This Page is Blank

Disclaimer

The information provided in *Mastering Productivity for Small Business Owners* is intended for general informational purposes only. While every effort has been made to ensure the accuracy and reliability of the content, the author and publisher do not guarantee the completeness, reliability, or suitability of the information provided for any particular purpose. Readers should consult with professionals or experts in specific areas, such as legal, financial, or business management, before making any decisions based on the information contained in this book.

The author and publisher are not liable for any losses, damages, or negative consequences that may arise from the use or reliance on the strategies, tools, or techniques described in this book. All information is provided "as is," and the reader assumes full responsibility for their actions based on the content.

Copyright

Acknowledgement

I would like to express my deepest gratitude to everyone who has contributed to the development of this book. First and foremost, I would like to thank the team at Crystal Coast HR for their unwavering support and commitment to excellence in human resources. Their expertise and dedication have been invaluable in shaping the insights shared here.

Special thanks also go to the countless business owners, managers, and HR professionals who have generously shared their experiences and challenges with me, offering real-world insights that have enriched the content. Your feedback has been instrumental in making this resource practical and relevant.

Lastly, I extend my heartfelt appreciation to my family and friends for their encouragement, patience, and understanding throughout the creation of this book.

This work would not have been possible without the contributions of all these wonderful individuals. Thank you.

Dedication

This book is dedicated to all the small business owners, entrepreneurs, and HR professionals who tirelessly work to build, grow, and nurture their companies. Your dedication to excellence, commitment to your teams, and relentless pursuit of success inspire me every day.

I also dedicate this work to my colleagues, mentors, and supporters at Crystal Coast HR, whose insights and guidance have shaped my understanding of the challenges and opportunities in the world of human resources.

May this resource serve as a tool to empower you in your journey toward increased productivity, efficiency, and success, making a lasting impact on your business and the lives of those you serve.

Table of Contents

Preface

Welcome to *Mastering Productivity for Small Business Owners*! As a small business owner, your time is your most precious resource. You juggle multiple responsibilities daily – managing operations, keeping customers satisfied, marketing your business, and striving to stay ahead of the competition. While the challenges may seem endless, the key to achieving sustainable success lies in your ability to master one essential skill: productivity.

This book is designed to be your roadmap for improving productivity in every aspect of your small business. Whether you're just starting out or looking to optimize your current operations, the strategies and tools presented here will help you streamline your workflow, reduce stress, and achieve more in less time.

Over the course of this book, we'll explore actionable time management techniques, productivity hacks, and powerful tools that will transform the way you approach your daily tasks. From setting clear goals to building a productive team culture and implementing effective systems, we'll guide you through the process of creating a well-oiled, high-functioning business. By leveraging technology, eliminating inefficiencies, and optimizing your routines, you'll have the resources to work smarter, not harder.

This book is not just about working harder or putting in more hours. It's about focusing your energy on what truly matters, making better decisions, and building the kind of productivity habits that lead to long-term success. It's about taking small, intentional steps each day to boost your efficiency and keep your business running smoothly – without sacrificing your well-being.

Inside, you'll find:

- **Time management techniques** to help you prioritize tasks and make the most of your day.

- **Streamlined workflows and processes** that reduce errors and enhance operational efficiency.

- **Automation tools and digital solutions** to handle repetitive tasks and free up time for creativity and growth.

- **Productivity hacks** that will help you stay focused, reduce distractions, and maximize your potential.

- **Tips for building a productive team culture** and encouraging collaboration across your business.

Each chapter is designed to provide you with practical, easy-to-implement advice that you can start using today. Along the way, you'll encounter real-world examples, success stories, and step-by-step guidance to help you build a more productive, efficient, and thriving business.

No matter what stage you're at in your business journey, remember that small changes can have a big impact. By making intentional decisions to prioritize productivity, you'll not only achieve more, but also gain the freedom and peace of mind you deserve as an entrepreneur.

I invite you to dive in, embrace these productivity principles, and begin taking action today. Let this book be the first step toward creating a more productive, profitable, and sustainable future for your small business.

Here's to your success!

David M Arnold, MS, SPHR
Crystal Coast HR | Crystal Coast Websites

Introduction

Purpose of the Book

Running a small business can be both exhilarating and challenging. As a small business owner, you juggle multiple roles—from managing operations to driving sales, handling customer relations, and keeping up with financial records. It's a never-ending cycle that can often leave you feeling overwhelmed and stretched thin. That's where productivity becomes a game-changer. By focusing on productivity, you can optimize your processes, save valuable time, and create a more efficient business that doesn't just survive but thrives.

The primary purpose of this book is to equip you with practical tools and strategies to boost your small business's productivity. Whether you're looking to streamline your workflow, enhance team collaboration, or simply make better use of your time, this book will provide you with actionable insights that you can implement right away.

Why focus on productivity, you might ask? The answer is simple: improving productivity directly impacts your bottom line. Efficient operations mean lower costs, quicker turnaround times, happier customers, and ultimately, higher profits. This is particularly crucial for small businesses, where resources are often limited, and every minute counts. By adopting productivity-enhancing practices, you can achieve more with less, giving you a competitive edge in your industry.

Moreover, in today's fast-paced digital world, staying productive isn't just about working harder—it's about working smarter. With the right productivity tools and techniques, you can automate mundane tasks, reduce time wastage, and free up your schedule for what truly matters—growing your business. This book will guide you through a comprehensive approach to enhancing productivity, helping you focus on what matters most and drive your business forward.

Who This book Is For

This book is designed for small business owners, entrepreneurs, and managers who are ready to take their business operations to the next level. Whether you're a seasoned business owner looking to refine your processes or a new entrepreneur just starting out, this guide offers something for everyone.

Here's who will benefit most from this book:

1. **Small Business Owners:** If you're wearing multiple hats and finding it hard to keep up, this book will help you streamline your processes, optimize your daily tasks, and achieve more with less effort. You'll learn how to leverage productivity tools to simplify your workload and reclaim valuable time.

2. **Entrepreneurs and Startups:** Starting a new business is both exciting and

challenging. This book provides essential strategies to help you build a strong foundation for productivity from the very beginning. By integrating these techniques early on, you can set your business up for long-term success.

3. **Managers and Team Leaders:** For those managing a team, ensuring everyone is on the same page and working efficiently is crucial. This book covers tools and techniques to boost team collaboration, enhance communication, and optimize project management, leading to a more productive work environment.

4. **Freelancers and Solopreneurs:** If you're running a one-person business, every minute is precious. This guide will show you how to automate repetitive tasks, manage your time effectively, and stay organized so you can focus on delivering high-quality work for your clients.

5. **Remote Business Owners:** In the era of remote work, managing productivity can be a bit more challenging. The tips and tools covered in this book are especially useful for those who operate their

businesses remotely, helping you maintain productivity even when working from home.

6. **Anyone Looking to Improve Efficiency:** If you're looking to optimize your day-to-day operations, cut down on time-wasting activities, and become more efficient in your work, this book is for you. The strategies discussed will help you unlock your full potential and achieve better results in less time.

What You'll Learn

This book is packed with valuable information designed to transform how you approach productivity in your small business. By the end of this guide, you'll have a deeper understanding of high-demand productivity tools, time management techniques, and workflow hacks that can streamline your operations. Here's a preview of what you'll discover:

1. **High-Demand Productivity Tools:** Learn about the latest and most effective productivity tools that are currently in high demand. We'll dive into tools that can help

you manage projects, enhance team collaboration, automate tasks, and keep your business running smoothly. Discover how tools like Asana, Trello, and Slack can revolutionize the way you work.

2. **Time Management Strategies:** Time is one of the most valuable assets for small business owners. This book will teach you proven time management techniques like the Pomodoro Technique, Time Blocking, and the Eisenhower Matrix. These strategies will help you prioritize tasks, reduce procrastination, and make the most out of every workday.

3. **Workflow Optimization Hacks:** Streamlining your workflow is key to increasing productivity. You'll learn how to automate repetitive tasks, set up efficient systems, and leverage technology to optimize your processes. Discover the power of tools like Zapier and IFTTT for creating automated workflows that save you hours every week.

4. **Boosting Team Productivity:** For businesses with teams, productivity isn't just about individual performance; it's

about how well the team works together. This book covers techniques for improving team collaboration, communication, and morale. You'll find out how to set clear goals, delegate effectively, and create a productive team culture.

5. **Reducing Operational Costs Through Efficiency:**
Efficiency doesn't just save time—it also saves money. Learn how to identify bottlenecks in your operations, reduce waste, and cut down on unnecessary expenses. We'll explore tools that can help you automate invoicing, inventory management, and other business processes, ultimately improving your bottom line.

6. **Implementing the Right Tools and Techniques for Your Business:**
Not all productivity tools and techniques are created equal, and what works for one business might not work for another. This book will guide you through the process of selecting the right tools that align with your specific business needs and goals. You'll gain insights into how to test, implement,

and evaluate different tools and techniques to find what works best for you.

7. **Practical Case Studies and Real-World Examples:**
   To bring these concepts to life, we'll include case studies and examples of small businesses that have successfully implemented these productivity strategies. These real-world stories will inspire you to apply the techniques in your own business and see tangible results.

8. **Future Trends in Small Business Productivity:**
   The landscape of productivity is constantly evolving, especially with advancements in technology. This book will explore upcoming trends in small business productivity, such as the rise of AI-driven tools, remote work productivity solutions, and more. Staying ahead of these trends can give your business a competitive edge.

Why This book is Your Go-To Productivity Resource

The insights and strategies shared in this book are backed by research, real-world experience, and proven best practices. Whether you're looking to make minor adjustments to your daily routine or implement major changes to your business processes, this guide provides the tools and knowledge you need to achieve your productivity goals.

The beauty of productivity lies in its versatility—it can be adapted and tailored to fit any business model. From solo entrepreneurs to small teams, every business can benefit from the principles outlined in this book. By investing in productivity, you're not just saving time and resources; you're investing in the long-term success and sustainability of your business.

How to Get the Most Out of This book

To fully benefit from the strategies discussed, we recommend taking a hands-on approach as you read through each chapter. Here are a few tips on how to make the most out of this book:

1. **Take Notes:** As you read, jot down ideas that resonate with you or highlight tools you're interested in trying.

2. **Implement One Strategy at a Time:** Focus on applying one productivity tool or technique before moving on to the next. This approach will prevent overwhelm and increase your chances of success.

3. **Customize Strategies to Fit Your Business:** Every business is unique. Use the guidelines provided in this book as a foundation, but don't be afraid to tweak the strategies to suit your specific needs.

4. **Set Measurable Goals:** Track your progress as you implement these productivity strategies. Set clear, measurable goals so you can see the impact on your business over time.

By the end of this book, you'll have a comprehensive toolkit of productivity techniques that can help transform your small business operations, making them more efficient, streamlined, and profitable. So let's dive in and start your journey to mastering productivity today!

Chapter 1: Understanding Productivity in Small Businesses

Defining Productivity

What Does Productivity Mean for Small Businesses?

At its core, productivity is the measure of how efficiently resources (like time, money, and labor) are used to produce a desired outcome. For large corporations, productivity might involve complex metrics, multi-layered departments, and large-scale systems. However, for small businesses, productivity is often about making the most out of limited resources to maximize results.

In the context of a small business, productivity means achieving more with less—optimizing operations to increase output without necessarily increasing the input. It's about streamlining processes, eliminating waste, and finding ways to work smarter, not harder. Whether you're a solo entrepreneur or managing a small team, improving productivity can make a significant difference in your day-to-day operations and long-term success.

Example: The Case of Sarah's Handmade Soap Business

Sarah runs a small handmade soap business from her home. She has a loyal customer base, but she often finds herself overwhelmed with fulfilling orders, managing social media, handling customer service, and keeping track of inventory. After assessing her productivity, Sarah realizes that her time is scattered across too many tasks, reducing her efficiency. By focusing on productivity, Sarah decides to streamline her processes by batching similar tasks together— like setting aside specific days for production, marketing, and administrative work. This simple change boosts her productivity, allowing her to fulfill more orders without increasing her workload.

This example highlights how small businesses can benefit from redefining productivity as a strategic approach to using their limited resources more effectively. By understanding productivity in the context of your business, you can begin to identify areas where improvements can be made to enhance efficiency and output.

The Impact of Productivity on Profitability

How Efficient Operations Lead to Cost Savings, Higher Revenue, and Sustainable Growth

For small businesses, improving productivity isn't just about getting things done faster; it's about enhancing the overall profitability of the business. Let's break down how productivity can directly impact your bottom line:

1. **Cost Savings**: Efficient operations reduce waste, whether it's time, materials, or money. By optimizing processes, you can cut down on unnecessary expenses, such as overtime costs, excessive inventory, or

unproductive labor hours. For example, adopting software for automated invoicing can reduce human error and save countless hours, translating to cost savings in administrative expenses.

2. **Higher Revenue**: When you streamline your workflow, you free up time that can be redirected towards revenue-generating activities, such as sales and marketing. By enhancing productivity, you can serve more clients, take on more projects, or increase your output without needing to hire additional staff.

Example: A local bakery used to manage its orders manually, which led to frequent errors and delayed deliveries. After implementing an online ordering system that streamlined the process, the bakery saw a 25% increase in orders and reduced mistakes by 40%. This productivity boost directly led to an increase in revenue and customer satisfaction.

3. **Sustainable Growth**: Productivity improvements lead to long-term benefits. Efficient operations build a solid foundation for growth. By optimizing your workflow and enhancing team

productivity, you can scale your business sustainably without overextending your resources.

Example: Consider a digital marketing agency that was struggling with project deadlines due to poor task management. By adopting a project management tool like Trello, they streamlined their workflow, met deadlines more consistently, and saw their client retention rate increase by 30%. This efficiency not only improved their profitability but also positioned them for sustainable growth.

The Productivity-Profitability Cycle

It's important to recognize that productivity and profitability feed into each other. The more efficient your operations, the more profit you generate. In turn, increased profitability allows you to reinvest in your business, whether it's upgrading your equipment, hiring skilled employees, or expanding your market reach. This creates a cycle of productivity leading to profitability, which then fuels further productivity improvements.

Common Productivity Challenges

Key Obstacles Small Business Owners Face

Despite the clear benefits of boosting productivity, small businesses often encounter unique challenges that can make it difficult to implement productivity strategies. Let's explore some of the most common productivity challenges and how they impact small businesses:

1. **Limited Resources**: Unlike large corporations, small businesses often have limited resources in terms of finances, manpower, and technology. This limitation can make it challenging to invest in productivity tools or additional staff that could ease the workload.

Example: A small graphic design studio wants to invest in advanced design software that could speed up project delivery. However, budget constraints prevent them from making this investment, leading to slower turnaround times.

2. **Time Constraints**: Time is a precious commodity for small business owners. Juggling multiple roles means that time management becomes critical. Without

proper time management strategies, small business owners may find themselves overwhelmed by the sheer volume of tasks, leading to burnout and decreased productivity.

Example: Tom, a freelance web developer, handles everything from coding to client communication and billing. Without a structured schedule, he often finds himself working late hours to meet deadlines, leaving little time for rest or strategic planning. This lack of time management affects both his productivity and well-being.

3. **Managing a Small Team**: For those who do have employees, managing a small team presents its own set of challenges. Ensuring that everyone is on the same page, motivated, and working efficiently can be difficult, especially without the right tools and systems in place.

Example: A small catering business with a team of five struggled with communication and task delegation, leading to errors in event planning. By introducing a team collaboration tool like Slack, they improved communication, reducing errors by 50% and increasing team productivity.

4. **Lack of Automation**: Many small businesses rely on manual processes for routine tasks, which can be time-consuming and prone to errors. Automating these tasks can significantly boost productivity, but many small business owners are either unaware of automation tools or reluctant to adopt new technologies.

Example: A small accounting firm was manually tracking expenses and generating reports, taking up to 10 hours a week. After switching to automated accounting software like QuickBooks, they cut this time down to 2 hours, freeing up 8 hours for other value-adding activities.

5. **Ineffective Time Management**: Without proper time management skills, small business owners may spend too much time on low-priority tasks, leaving important activities unattended. Tools like the Eisenhower Matrix or Time Blocking can help prioritize tasks more effectively.

Example: A local boutique owner was spending hours on social media marketing without clear results, neglecting inventory management and customer engagement. By using a time management strategy like the Pomodoro Technique, she was able to allocate dedicated time slots for different activities, improving overall productivity.

6. **Resistance to Change**: Adopting new productivity tools or strategies often requires a change in habits, which can be challenging. Business owners and employees alike may be resistant to changing their workflow, even if it means long-term benefits.

Example: A small legal firm was hesitant to move from physical document management to a cloud-based system due to concerns over security and a steep learning curve. However, once they transitioned, they found that document retrieval time was cut by 70%, significantly boosting productivity.

Strategies to Overcome Common Productivity Challenges

Solution 1: Leverage Technology to Maximize Efficiency

While small businesses may have limited resources, there are many affordable or even free tools available that can significantly boost productivity. Tools like Trello for project management, Hootsuite for social media scheduling, and Google Workspace for collaboration can streamline operations without breaking the bank.

Solution 2: Prioritize Time Management Training

Time management is a skill that can be developed. By investing in time management training for yourself and your team, you can ensure that everyone is working efficiently. Techniques like Time Blocking and the Pomodoro Technique can help structure your day for maximum productivity.

Solution 3: Automate Repetitive Tasks

Automation is a powerful tool for saving time and reducing human error. For example, automating your email marketing through tools like Mailchimp or automating invoicing with tools like FreshBooks can free up valuable hours every week.

Solution 4: Foster a Collaborative Team Environment

For businesses with a small team, fostering collaboration is key to productivity. Tools like

Asana for project management and Slack for communication can help keep everyone on the same page, ensuring tasks are completed efficiently and on time.

Solution 5: Embrace Change and Continuous Learning

Adopting new tools and strategies may require an initial investment of time and effort, but the long-term benefits are worth it. Encourage a culture of continuous improvement in your business by regularly assessing productivity and being open to new solutions.

Chapter Summary

In this chapter, we've explored what productivity means for small businesses and why it's a crucial component of success. We discussed how productivity impacts profitability by reducing costs, increasing revenue, and supporting sustainable growth. We also delved into common productivity challenges faced by small business owners, including limited resources, time constraints, and managing small teams.

By understanding these challenges and adopting strategies to overcome them, you can boost your business's efficiency, streamline operations, and achieve greater profitability. As we move forward, the next chapters will dive deeper into specific productivity tools, time management techniques, and workflow hacks that can help you take your small business to the next level.

In the following chapter, we will explore **high-demand productivity tools** that are designed to optimize your business operations and help you achieve your goals faster. Let's dive in!

Chapter 2: Essential Productivity Tools for Small Businesses

In today's fast-paced business environment, leveraging the right productivity tools can make all the difference in running an efficient and successful small business. These tools not only help streamline operations but also save valuable time, reduce costs, and improve overall team collaboration. This chapter will introduce you to some of the most popular and high-demand productivity tools available today, providing practical examples of how they can be integrated into your business to boost efficiency.

Project Management Tools

Managing projects, tasks, and deadlines can be a major challenge for small business owners, especially when resources are limited. Project management tools are designed to help you organize your work, track progress, and ensure that projects are completed on time and within budget.

1. Asana

Overview: Asana is a versatile project management tool that allows you to create tasks, assign them to team members, set deadlines, and track progress. It is ideal for managing both individual and team projects.

Features:

- Task creation and assignment
- Due dates and reminders
- Project timelines and progress tracking
- Customizable project templates
- Integrations with other apps like Slack and Google Workspace

Example:
Imagine a small marketing agency that handles

multiple client campaigns simultaneously. The team uses Asana to organize each campaign into a project, breaking down tasks like content creation, social media scheduling, and client reporting. Each task is assigned to a team member with a set deadline. As a result, the team has a clear overview of who is responsible for what, ensuring that all deliverables are completed on time.

2. Trello

Overview: Trello uses a visual board and card system to organize tasks and projects. It's especially popular among small businesses for its simplicity and flexibility.

Features:

- Drag-and-drop interface with boards, lists, and cards

- Task assignment and due dates

- Checklists and attachments

- Integration with apps like Slack, Dropbox, and Google Drive

- Automation through Trello's Butler feature

Example:

A local event planning business uses Trello to manage all aspects of their event preparation. Each event has its own Trello board, with lists for planning stages such as "To Do," "In Progress," and "Completed." Cards within these lists represent tasks like booking venues, arranging catering, and sending out invitations. The visual layout helps the team stay on top of deadlines and ensures nothing falls through the cracks.

3. Monday.com

Overview: Monday.com is a robust project management platform that focuses on collaboration and customization. It's ideal for teams looking for a more structured approach to project management.

Features:

- Customizable workflows and templates

- Timeline and Gantt chart views

- Time tracking and automation

- Integration with tools like Slack, Zoom, and Microsoft Teams

- Reporting and analytics

Example:

A software development startup uses Monday.com to manage its product development lifecycle. The team creates custom workflows for each phase of the project, from initial planning to coding, testing, and deployment. With Monday.com's time tracking feature, the team can monitor how much time is spent on each task, allowing them to optimize their processes and meet client deadlines more efficiently.

Communication and Collaboration Tools

Effective communication is key to productivity, especially for small businesses with remote or hybrid teams. Communication and collaboration tools can help streamline conversations, reduce email overload, and keep everyone connected.

1. Slack

Overview: Slack is a popular messaging platform designed for team communication and collaboration. It offers real-time messaging, file sharing, and integrations with various productivity tools.

Features:

- Channels for organizing conversations by topics or projects

- Direct messaging and group chats

- Integration with apps like Asana, Trello, and Google Drive

- File sharing and searchable message history

- Video and voice call functionality

Example:
A boutique consulting firm uses Slack to keep their remote team connected. They have channels dedicated to different projects, where team members can share updates, ask questions, and collaborate in real-time. By reducing the need for lengthy email threads, Slack helps the team stay focused and responsive.

2. Microsoft Teams

Overview: Microsoft Teams is a collaboration tool that combines chat, video conferencing, file sharing, and app integrations, making it ideal for businesses already using Microsoft 365.

Features:

- Video and voice calls

- Chat channels and direct messaging

- Integration with Microsoft Office apps (Word, Excel, PowerPoint)

- File sharing and collaboration in real-time

- Meeting scheduling and recording

Example:

A financial advisory firm uses Microsoft Teams to conduct virtual meetings with clients and internal team members. The integration with Microsoft Office allows them to collaborate on documents during meetings, making it easy to share reports, presentations, and financial statements in real-time.

3. Zoom

Overview: Zoom is one of the most widely used video conferencing tools, known for its reliability and ease of use. It's perfect for hosting virtual meetings, webinars, and online training sessions.

Features:

- HD video and audio quality

- Screen sharing and recording

- Breakout rooms for group discussions

- Integration with Google Calendar and Outlook

- Virtual backgrounds and filters

Example:

A small coaching business uses Zoom to conduct online sessions with clients. The screen sharing feature allows the coach to present slides and resources, while breakout rooms are used for interactive group exercises during workshops.

Automation and Workflow Tools

Automation tools can help small businesses save time by handling repetitive tasks, freeing up resources for more strategic activities.

1. Zapier

Overview: Zapier connects different apps and automates workflows, allowing you to create "Zaps" that trigger actions between apps without any coding.

Features:

- Connects over 5,000 apps (e.g., Gmail, Slack, Trello)
- Automated workflows for repetitive tasks
- Custom triggers and actions
- Multi-step Zaps for complex workflows

Example:
A small e-commerce store uses Zapier to automate their order processing. When a new order is placed on Shopify, Zapier automatically adds the customer details to a Google Sheet, sends a confirmation email via Gmail, and updates the inventory in QuickBooks, saving the owner hours of manual work each week.

2. IFTTT (If This Then That)

Overview: IFTTT allows you to create simple automation workflows between different apps and devices using "If This, Then That" logic.

Features:

- Over 700 integrations with apps and smart devices

- Simple automation recipes (e.g., "If I receive an email, then save the attachment to Dropbox")
- Applets for personal and business use

Example:

A digital marketing freelancer uses IFTTT to streamline social media posting. When a new blog post is published on WordPress, IFTTT automatically shares it across multiple social media platforms like Twitter, LinkedIn, and Facbook, increasing visibility without manual effort.

Document Management and Cloud Storage

Efficient document management is essential for collaboration, security, and accessibility. Cloud storage solutions enable small businesses to store, share, and collaborate on files in real-time.

1. Google Workspace

Overview: Google Workspace (formerly G Suite) offers cloud-based productivity tools like Google Drive, Docs, Sheets, and Slides, enabling real-time collaboration.

Features:

- Secure cloud storage with Google Drive

- Real-time collaboration on documents

- Integration with Gmail, Calendar, and other Google apps

- Advanced sharing permissions and access controls

- Video conferencing with Google Meet

Example:
A small architecture firm uses Google Workspace to collaborate on design plans with clients. Team members can work on the same Google Doc or Sheet simultaneously, making real-time edits and comments, which streamlines the revision process and improves client satisfaction.

2. Dropbox

Overview: Dropbox is a cloud storage solution known for its simplicity and powerful file-sharing capabilities.

Features:

- File storage and sharing

- Advanced file versioning and recovery
- Integration with Microsoft Office and Slack
- Team folders and access controls
- Offline access to files

Example:

A photography business uses Dropbox to store and share high-resolution images with clients. The ability to create shared folders with restricted access ensures that sensitive client photos remain secure while still being easily accessible.

Customer Relationship Management (CRM) Systems

A CRM system helps small businesses manage interactions with current and potential customers, track sales leads, and improve customer service.

1. HubSpot

Overview: HubSpot CRM is a free, user-friendly CRM platform that offers features for sales, marketing, and customer service.

Features:

- Contact and lead management

- Email tracking and automation

- Sales pipeline management

- Marketing automation (e.g., email campaigns)

- Reporting and analytics

Example:
A small IT services company uses HubSpot to track leads and automate follow-up emails. By managing their sales pipeline more effectively, they increased their lead conversion rate by 20%.

2. Zoho CRM

Overview: Zoho CRM is a customizable platform that helps businesses streamline their sales, marketing, and support processes.

Features:

- Lead and contact management

- Workflow automation

- Social media integration

- AI-powered analytics and predictions

- Mobile app for on-the-go access

Example:
A real estate agency uses Zoho CRM to manage client interactions, automate property follow-ups, and send personalized newsletters. This helps them stay top-of-mind with potential buyers and sellers.

3. Salesforce

Overview: Salesforce is a leading CRM platform known for its scalability and advanced features, making it suitable for small businesses with growth ambitions.

Features:

- Comprehensive contact management

- Advanced reporting and analytics

- Marketing automation and campaign management

- Integration with third-party apps

- AI-powered insights with Salesforce Einstein

Example:
A startup that specializes in SaaS solutions uses Salesforce to manage its customer onboarding

process. The automation of follow-up emails and data-driven insights help improve customer retention rates, leading to steady business growth.

Conclusion

Investing in the right productivity tools is crucial for small businesses looking to optimize operations, improve team collaboration, and enhance customer satisfaction. From project management platforms like Asana and Trello to communication tools like Slack and Zoom, each of these tools offers unique benefits tailored to different business needs.

By integrating these tools into your workflow, you can not only streamline day-to-day tasks but also gain a competitive edge in your industry. Whether you're a solopreneur or managing a small team, the right combination of productivity tools can transform the way you do business, leading to increased efficiency and profitability.

As we move forward to the next chapter, we will explore **strategic marketing tools** to help small businesses attract and retain customers. Stay tuned!

Chapter 3: Time Management Techniques for Small Business Owners

Effective time management is the backbone of productivity, especially for small business owners who often juggle multiple responsibilities. Managing your time well not only boosts efficiency but also reduces stress, enabling you to focus on growth and long-term goals. This chapter delves into essential time management techniques that can transform how you work, helping you achieve more in less time. We'll explore prioritization frameworks, scheduling strategies, and productivity hacks to help you make the most of every minute.

The Importance of Time Management

Time is one of the most valuable resources for any small business owner. Unlike money or resources, you can't get back lost time. Effective time management allows you to allocate your hours wisely, focusing on what truly matters for your business. Poor time management can lead to missed deadlines, low productivity, and increased stress, all of which can impact your business's bottom line.

Key Benefits of Time Management:

1. **Increased Productivity**: When you manage your time effectively, you can accomplish more tasks in less time, freeing up hours for strategic planning or personal activities.

2. **Reduced Stress**: A well-organized schedule helps reduce the feeling of being overwhelmed, as you know exactly what needs to be done and when.

3. **Improved Decision-Making**: Prioritizing tasks allows you to focus on high-impact activities, leading to better decision-making and business outcomes.

4. **Work-Life Balance**: Efficient time management helps you strike a balance between work and personal life, reducing the risk of burnout.

Example:

A small bakery owner found herself constantly overwhelmed by day-to-day operations, from inventory management to customer orders. By implementing time management techniques like scheduling and prioritization, she was able to delegate tasks more effectively, resulting in smoother operations and more time to focus on expanding her business.

Prioritization Frameworks

Prioritizing tasks is crucial for small business owners who often wear many hats. Knowing what to tackle first can save you time and help you focus on activities that drive growth.

1. The Eisenhower Matrix

The Eisenhower Matrix, also known as the Urgent-Important Matrix, helps you categorize tasks based on their urgency and importance. It's divided into four quadrants:

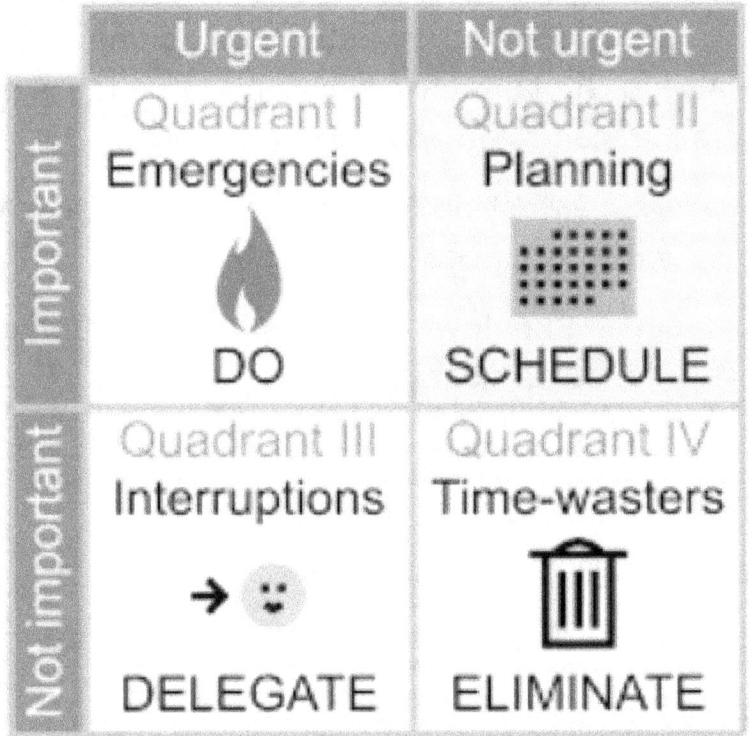

Example:

A freelance graphic designer uses the Eisenhower Matrix to prioritize her workload. Client deadlines fall into Quadrant 1, while skill development and networking go into Quadrant 2. Responding to non-critical emails is categorized in Quadrant 3, and social media scrolling falls into Quadrant 4. This approach ensures she focuses on what matters most to her business growth.

2. The ABCDE Method

The ABCDE Method, popularized by Brian Tracy, is a simple but effective way to prioritize tasks by labeling them:

- **A**: Must-do tasks with severe consequences if not completed
- **B**: Should-do tasks with minor consequences if delayed
- **C**: Nice-to-do tasks with no real consequences
- **D**: Delegate these tasks if possible
- **E**: Eliminate unnecessary tasks altogether

Example:
A marketing consultant uses the ABCDE Method to organize her to-do list each morning. Tasks like client presentations are marked "A," while attending optional webinars are marked "C." This method allows her to focus her energy on high-priority activities that directly impact client satisfaction and revenue.

Time Blocking and Scheduling

Time blocking is a technique where you schedule specific blocks of time for different tasks or activities throughout the day. This method is effective for avoiding distractions and ensuring that your time is dedicated to what's most important.

How to Implement Time Blocking:

1. **Identify Your Priorities**: Start by listing out all your tasks for the week.

2. **Allocate Time Slots**: Dedicate specific time slots for each task, including breaks.

3. **Stick to Your Schedule**: Treat each block as a meeting with yourself—show up on time and focus only on the task at hand.

Example:

A small business owner who runs a boutique uses time blocking to manage her day. From 9-11 AM, she focuses on customer orders, from 11-12 PM on inventory updates, and from 2-4 PM on marketing efforts. By dedicating specific times for each task, she reduces multitasking and increases efficiency.

Benefits of Time Blocking:

- **Improves Focus**: By dedicating uninterrupted time to each task, you reduce the risk of getting sidetracked.

- **Reduces Decision Fatigue**: Knowing what to work on and when to work on it eliminates the need for constant decision-making throughout the day.

- **Increases Productivity**: It helps you accomplish more by optimizing your time allocation.

The Pomodoro Technique

The Pomodoro Technique is a time management method developed by Francesco Cirillo in the late 1980s. It involves breaking work into intervals, typically 25 minutes long, separated by short breaks. This approach helps maintain focus and prevent burnout.

How to Use the Pomodoro Technique:

1. **Set a Timer for 25 Minutes**: Work on a single task until the timer goes off.

2. **Take a 5-Minute Break**: Step away from your workspace to relax.

3. **Repeat**: After four cycles, take a longer break (15-30 minutes).

Example:

A social media manager finds herself getting easily distracted by notifications and emails. By using the Pomodoro Technique, she sets 25-minute intervals to focus solely on content creation, followed by 5-minute breaks to check emails. This approach significantly boosts her productivity and keeps her tasks on track.

Benefits of the Pomodoro Technique:

- **Improves Concentration**: Short work intervals help maintain focus without feeling overwhelmed.

- **Boosts Motivation**: Knowing a break is coming soon can make it easier to push through challenging tasks.

- **Reduces Mental Fatigue**: Frequent breaks help refresh your mind, reducing the risk of burnout.

Eliminating Time Wasters

Time wasters are activities that do not add value to your business. Identifying and eliminating these distractions can free up valuable time for more productive work.

Common Time Wasters:

1. **Email Overload**: Constantly checking and responding to emails can eat into your productive hours. Instead, set specific times during the day to check your inbox.

Example:
A small business owner in the fashion industry found herself spending over two hours daily on emails. By setting designated email check-in times (e.g., 10 AM and 4 PM), she cut this down to 30 minutes, freeing up time for designing new collections.

2. **Social Media Distractions**: While social media can be a powerful marketing tool, it can also be a major time sink. Use social media scheduling tools like Buffer or Hootsuite to plan and automate posts.

Example:
A digital marketing consultant uses Buffer to

schedule a week's worth of social media content in one sitting. This allows her to focus on other tasks throughout the week without getting sucked into endless scrolling.

3. **Unproductive Meetings**: Meetings can be one of the biggest productivity killers if not managed well. Only schedule meetings when absolutely necessary, and keep them short and focused with a clear agenda.

Example:
A tech startup founder noticed that weekly meetings were dragging on, taking up valuable time. By implementing a 15-minute daily stand-up meeting format, the team stayed aligned on priorities while freeing up hours for coding and product development.

Strategies to Eliminate Time Wasters:

- **Use the Two-Minute Rule**: If a task takes less than two minutes, do it immediately. Otherwise, schedule it.

- **Batch Similar Tasks**: Group similar tasks together, like phone calls or admin work, to complete them in one focused session.

- **Leverage Automation**: Use automation tools like Zapier to handle repetitive tasks, freeing up your time for more strategic work.

Conclusion

Time management is a critical skill for small business owners looking to maximize their productivity and streamline operations. By implementing techniques like prioritization frameworks, time blocking, and the Pomodoro Technique, you can take control of your schedule and reduce the stress of running a business.

The key is to find a combination of strategies that works best for you and your team. Whether it's using the Eisenhower Matrix to prioritize tasks or adopting time blocking to structure your day, the goal is to make the most of your limited time. Remember, effective time management is not just about doing more; it's about focusing on what truly matters and using your time wisely.

In the next chapter, we'll explore **workflow optimization hacks** that can further streamline your business processes and boost efficiency. Stay tuned!

Chapter 4: Streamlining Workflows and Processes

As a small business owner, you often face the challenge of wearing multiple hats— managing operations, marketing, customer service, and more. The key to staying productive and efficient in this environment is streamlining your workflows and processes. Optimizing these areas not only improves efficiency but also reduces errors, saves time, and ultimately boosts your bottom line. In this chapter, we'll explore the benefits of streamlined workflows, how to create Standard Operating Procedures (SOPs), the power of the 80/20 Rule (Pareto

Principle), and the strategic use of delegation and outsourcing.

The Benefits of Streamlined Workflows

Streamlining workflows means optimizing your processes to ensure that tasks are completed more efficiently and with fewer errors. A streamlined workflow reduces redundancies, automates repetitive tasks, and clarifies roles and responsibilities, allowing your team to focus on high-value activities.

Key Benefits of Streamlined Workflows:

1. **Improved Efficiency**: By eliminating unnecessary steps and automating routine tasks, you can reduce the time it takes to complete projects. This leads to faster delivery times, which is particularly beneficial in competitive industries.

Example:
A small e-commerce store reduced its order processing time by integrating an automated order fulfillment system. Instead of manually inputting orders, the system automatically synced with their online store, generating

shipping labels and updating inventory in real time. This streamlined workflow cut down order fulfillment time by 50%, leading to faster deliveries and happier customers.

2. **Reduced Errors**: When workflows are standardized, there's less room for human error. This is particularly important for tasks like invoicing, inventory management, and customer communication, where mistakes can have significant consequences.

Example:
An accounting firm implemented a checklist system for client audits, which standardized the process across all team members. This not only improved accuracy but also reduced the time spent double-checking each other's work, cutting down errors by 30%.

3. **Cost Savings**: Streamlined workflows reduce the need for manual labor, freeing up resources and lowering operational costs. This can lead to significant savings, especially for small businesses with tight budgets.

Example:

A local restaurant used to manually schedule staff shifts, leading to frequent scheduling conflicts and overtime pay. By adopting scheduling software, the owner saved over $1,000 per month in labor costs and reduced scheduling errors.

4. **Enhanced Team Collaboration**: Clear workflows help ensure that everyone knows their responsibilities, which can improve team collaboration and communication. When team members are on the same page, projects run more smoothly.

Example:

A digital marketing agency implemented a project management tool to track client campaigns. This allowed the team to see real-time updates, set deadlines, and assign tasks, leading to better collaboration and timely project delivery.

Standard Operating Procedures (SOPs)

Creating Standard Operating Procedures (SOPs) is one of the most effective ways to streamline your workflows. SOPs are detailed, step-by-step instructions on how to perform specific tasks. They ensure consistency, reduce training time, and help maintain quality across the board.

Benefits of SOPs:

- **Consistency**: SOPs ensure that tasks are completed the same way every time, leading to consistent quality and outcomes.

- **Reduced Training Time**: New employees can quickly get up to speed by following SOPs, reducing the time needed for training.

- **Improved Accountability**: SOPs clarify roles and responsibilities, making it easier to hold team members accountable for their work.

How to Create Effective SOPs:

1. **Identify Key Processes**: Focus on recurring tasks that are critical to your business, such as customer onboarding, order fulfillment, or social media management.

2. **Document the Steps**: Write clear, concise steps for each task. Use bullet points, numbered lists, or flowcharts to make the instructions easy to follow.

3. **Include Visuals**: Screenshots, diagrams, or videos can enhance understanding, especially for complex tasks.

4. **Review and Update Regularly**: SOPs should be living documents that evolve as your business grows. Regularly review and update them to reflect changes in processes or tools.

Example:

A small web development agency created SOPs for its website launch process, from initial client meetings to final deployment. The SOPs included checklists for each phase, ensuring that no steps were missed. As a result, project delivery times improved by 20%, and client satisfaction increased.

The 80/20 Rule (Pareto Principle)

The 80/20 Rule, also known as the Pareto Principle, states that 80% of your results come from 20% of your efforts. For small business owners, this means that a small portion of your tasks or clients may be driving the majority of your revenue and growth. By identifying and focusing on these high-impact areas, you can optimize your productivity and profitability.

How to Apply the 80/20 Rule:

1. **Identify High-Impact Tasks**: Analyze your business activities to determine which tasks or clients generate the most value. This could include top-selling products, high-paying clients, or marketing channels that drive the most traffic.

Example:
A freelance writer analyzed her client base and discovered that 20% of her clients generated 80% of her income. She decided to focus more on these high-value clients, offering premium services and packages, which increased her monthly revenue by 30%.

2. **Eliminate Low-Value Activities**: Once you've identified your high-impact tasks, look for activities that take up time but don't contribute much to your bottom line.

Consider delegating, automating, or eliminating these tasks.

Example:
A local gym owner realized that social media posts were taking up too much time without driving significant engagement. By outsourcing social media management, he was able to focus on client retention and member acquisition, which had a more direct impact on revenue.

3. **Focus on Your Strengths**: The 80/20 Rule also applies to personal productivity. Focus on tasks that align with your strengths and delegate the rest.

Example:
An interior designer focused on client consultations and design work, which were her strengths, while outsourcing administrative tasks like bookkeeping to a virtual assistant. This shift allowed her to take on more projects and increase her revenue.

Delegating and Outsourcing

As a small business owner, you might be tempted to do everything yourself to save costs.

However, trying to handle everything can lead to burnout and inefficiency. Delegating and outsourcing tasks can free up your time for core business activities that drive growth.

The Benefits of Delegating and Outsourcing:

- **Increased Efficiency**: By delegating routine tasks, you can focus on strategic initiatives that require your expertise.

- **Access to Specialized Skills**: Outsourcing allows you to tap into the skills of experts, which can improve the quality of your work.

- **Scalability**: Delegating tasks can help you scale your business more quickly by freeing up your time for growth-oriented activities.

What to Delegate or Outsource:

1. **Administrative Tasks**: Tasks like data entry, email management, and appointment scheduling can be easily delegated to a virtual assistant.

Example:
A real estate agent hired a virtual assistant to manage her inbox, schedule appointments, and

update listings. This freed up 10 hours a week, allowing her to focus on closing deals and growing her client base.

2. **Marketing and Social Media**: If managing your online presence is eating into your time, consider outsourcing to a digital marketing agency.

Example:
A small bakery outsourced its social media marketing to a local agency. Within three months, their Instagram followers doubled, and in-store foot traffic increased by 25%.

3. **Accounting and Bookkeeping**: Managing finances can be time-consuming and complex. Outsourcing to a professional accountant can save time and reduce errors.

Example:
A tech startup outsourced its accounting to a CPA firm, which handled tax filings, payroll, and financial reporting. This allowed the founders to focus on product development and fundraising.

How to Delegate Effectively:

- **Identify the Right Tasks**: Focus on delegating low-value or repetitive tasks that don't require your direct input.

- **Choose the Right People**: Whether hiring a freelancer, agency, or virtual assistant, make sure they have the skills and experience needed for the job.

- **Provide Clear Instructions**: Set clear expectations, provide detailed instructions, and establish deadlines to ensure tasks are completed to your satisfaction.

- **Use Project Management Tools**: Tools like Asana or Trello can help you track delegated tasks and monitor progress.

Conclusion

Streamlining workflows and processes is essential for small business owners looking to boost productivity and reduce operational inefficiencies. By leveraging tools like SOPs, prioritizing high-impact tasks using the 80/20 Rule, and strategically delegating or outsourcing, you can free up valuable time and resources to focus on growing your business.

The key is to continually evaluate and optimize your processes. As your business evolves, so should your workflows. Regularly reviewing and updating your strategies ensures that you stay ahead of the competition and remain agile in a rapidly changing market.

In the next chapter, we'll explore **advanced automation techniques** that can further enhance your productivity and help you stay competitive. Get ready to take your business operations to the next level!

Chapter 5: Leveraging Technology to Automate and Optimize

In today's fast-paced digital landscape, small businesses need to leverage technology to stay competitive. One of the most effective ways to enhance productivity is through automation. By automating repetitive tasks, streamlining accounting and finance processes, managing inventory, and optimizing digital marketing, you can save time, reduce costs, and focus on scaling your business. In this chapter, we'll explore various tools and techniques that can help you automate your operations, providing practical examples to show how these technologies can transform your business.

Automating Repetitive Tasks

Automation is a game-changer for small businesses. It allows you to offload mundane, time-consuming tasks to software, freeing up your time to focus on strategic activities. Automation tools can handle everything from invoicing to email marketing and social media posting.

Key Areas for Automation:

1. **Invoicing and Payments**
   Manual invoicing can be tedious and prone to errors, especially as your customer base grows. Automated invoicing tools can streamline this process, ensuring timely and accurate billing.

Example:
A freelance graphic designer used to spend hours each month creating invoices and following up on payments. By switching to **FreshBooks**, she automated the invoicing process, enabling automatic payment reminders and recurring invoices for retainer

clients. This change reduced her admin time by 60%, allowing her to take on more client work.

2. **Email   Marketing**
   Keeping in touch with customers is crucial for maintaining engagement, but crafting and sending emails manually can be time-consuming. Tools like **Mailchimp** and **Constant Contact** automate email marketing, allowing you to schedule campaigns, segment your audience, and track performance.

Example:
A local gym wanted to increase membership renewals and engagement. By using Mailchimp, they set up automated email campaigns to send personalized workout tips, membership reminders, and promotional offers based on user preferences. As a result, they saw a 20% increase in renewals and a 15% boost in class attendance.

3. **Social   Media   Management**
   Maintaining an active presence on social media is essential for brand visibility, but posting consistently across multiple platforms can be overwhelming. Social media automation tools like **Hootsuite**

and **Buffer** allow you to schedule posts in advance, monitor engagement, and analyze performance metrics.

Example:

A boutique clothing store used Hootsuite to plan and schedule posts for Instagram, Facbook, and Twitter. By batching content creation and automating posts, they saved several hours each week and saw a 25% increase in social media engagement.

4. **Customer Support**

   Automating customer support with chatbots and automated response systems can improve customer satisfaction while reducing the workload on your support team. Tools like **Zendesk** and **Intercom** enable automated ticketing, FAQs, and live chat support.

Example:

An online electronics retailer implemented a chatbot on their website to handle common customer queries like order status and return policies. This reduced the volume of support tickets by 40% and improved response times for complex issues.

Accounting and Finance Tools

Managing finances is critical for any small business, but it can be time-consuming and complex. Automating accounting and bookkeeping processes can help you stay on top of your finances with minimal effort.

Recommended Accounting Tools:

1. **QuickBooks**

   QuickBooks is one of the most popular accounting tools for small businesses. It offers features like invoicing, expense tracking, payroll management, and financial reporting, all in one platform.

Example:
A home-based bakery used to manage their finances manually with spreadsheets. After switching to QuickBooks, they were able to automate invoice generation, track expenses, and generate profit and loss statements. This saved them several hours each week and improved their cash flow management.

2. **FreshBooks**

   FreshBooks is ideal for freelancers and

service-based businesses. It simplifies invoicing, expense tracking, time tracking, and reporting, making it easier to manage your finances.

Example:

A small marketing consultancy struggled with tracking billable hours for multiple clients. By adopting FreshBooks, they automated time tracking and invoice generation, which reduced billing errors and increased revenue by ensuring all billable hours were accounted for.

3. **Expensify**

   For businesses with frequent travel or expense reports, **Expensify** automates the process of tracking receipts, mileage, and reimbursements. It integrates with accounting software like QuickBooks for seamless financial management.

Example:

A consulting firm used Expensify to manage travel expenses for their team. By automating expense reporting and integrating with QuickBooks, they cut down the time spent on processing reimbursements by 50%.

Inventory Management Systems

Efficient inventory management is crucial for businesses that deal with physical products. Automating inventory management helps you track stock levels, prevent overstocking or stockouts, and streamline order fulfillment.

Top Inventory Management Tools:

1. **Square for Retail**
   Square offers an all-in-one point-of-sale (POS) system that includes inventory management features. It's perfect for small businesses looking to integrate sales and inventory tracking.

Example:

A small toy store used to manage inventory manually, which led to frequent stockouts of popular items. After implementing Square, they automated inventory tracking, received low-stock alerts, and optimized reordering processes. This resulted in a 15% increase in sales due to better product availability.

2. **TradeGecko (now QuickBooks Commerce)**
   TradeGecko is a robust inventory management tool designed for growing

businesses. It offers features like order management, demand forecasting, and multi-channel integration.

Example:

An online fashion boutique used TradeGecko to sync inventory across their Shopify store, Amazon, and physical retail location. This automation eliminated discrepancies in stock levels and streamlined order fulfillment, reducing shipping errors by 30%.

3. **Zoho**   **Inventory**

   Zoho Inventory is a powerful tool for managing inventory, orders, and shipping. It integrates with popular e-commerce platforms and shipping carriers.

Example:

A health supplements business automated its inventory management with Zoho Inventory, which integrated with their Shopify store. This enabled them to manage product batches and expiration dates, resulting in a 20% reduction in product waste.

Digital Marketing Tools

Marketing is essential for business growth, but it can be time-consuming. Leveraging automation tools can help you scale your digital marketing efforts efficiently.

Popular Digital Marketing Tools:

1. **Hootsuite**
   Hootsuite is a social media management tool that allows you to schedule posts, track performance, and manage multiple social media accounts from one dashboard.

Example:
A small real estate agency used Hootsuite to schedule property listings, market updates, and customer testimonials on social media. This consistent posting strategy helped them grow their social media following by 40% in six months.

2. **Mailchimp**
   Mailchimp is an all-in-one email marketing platform that automates email campaigns, audience segmentation, and analytics. It's great for nurturing leads and converting customers.

Example:

A local spa used Mailchimp to set up automated email sequences for new subscribers. They offered a 10% discount on first appointments, which increased bookings by 25%.

3. **Canva for Content Creation**
   While not strictly an automation tool, Canva streamlines the process of creating professional graphics for social media, marketing materials, and ads.

Example:

A small non-profit used Canva to quickly design event flyers, social media graphics, and donor reports. The user-friendly templates saved them significant time, allowing them to focus more on fundraising efforts.

Benefits of Leveraging Technology for Automation

1. **Time Savings**: Automating repetitive tasks frees up time for high-value activities that contribute to business growth.

2. **Cost Reduction**: Automation can reduce labor costs by minimizing manual work and increasing efficiency.

3. **Scalability**: Automation tools enable you to handle higher volumes of work without increasing overhead.

4. **Improved Accuracy**: Reducing manual input lowers the risk of errors, leading to better data accuracy and decision-making.

Conclusion

Leveraging technology to automate and optimize your business processes can lead to significant gains in productivity, efficiency, and profitability. By automating repetitive tasks, managing finances with accounting tools, optimizing inventory with dedicated systems, and scaling your marketing efforts through digital tools, you can create a more agile and competitive business.

The key to success is choosing the right tools that align with your business needs. Start small, automate one process at a time, and measure the impact. As you grow more comfortable with automation, you can expand its use across other areas of your business.

In the next chapter, we will delve into **advanced data analytics and performance tracking**, exploring how small businesses can harness data to make informed decisions and drive growth. Get ready to unlock the power of data in your business journey!

Chapter 6: Productivity Hacks for Small Business Owners

Small business owners often juggle multiple roles—manager, marketer, accountant, and more. With so many responsibilities, finding ways to maximize productivity is crucial. In this chapter, we'll explore some practical productivity hacks that can help you streamline your daily operations, manage your time better, and ultimately boost your business's performance. From batch processing and using templates to adopting mindfulness practices, these techniques are designed to help you work smarter, not harder.

Batch Processing

Batch processing is a powerful technique that involves grouping similar tasks together to complete them in a single session. This approach reduces the time lost to context switching, which can disrupt your flow and decrease productivity.

Why Batch Processing Works

When you switch between different types of tasks—like responding to emails, making phone calls, and working on a project—your brain needs time to adjust. This context switching can lead to mental fatigue and reduced efficiency. By batching similar tasks, you can stay focused on one type of work, leading to faster completion times and improved concentration.

Examples of Batch Processing

1. **Email Management**
   Instead of checking your email every time a notification pops up, set aside specific times of the day to go through your inbox. For example, you can schedule two 30-

minute sessions in the morning and afternoon to read and respond to emails.

Example:

A digital marketing consultant used to check her emails constantly throughout the day, which disrupted her workflow. By switching to a batch processing approach, she only checked emails at 10 AM and 4 PM. This change increased her productivity, allowing her to focus on client projects without distractions.

2. **Social Media Content Creation**
   Creating and posting social media content can be time-consuming. By batching this process, you can create all your social media posts for the week in one sitting, schedule them using a tool like **Buffer** or **Hootsuite**, and free up time for other activities.

Example:

A fitness coach spent several hours each week creating daily social media posts. By dedicating every Monday morning to batch-create and schedule all her posts for the week, she saved over three hours per week, which she reinvested in client training sessions.

3. **Invoicing and Financial Reports**
   Instead of processing invoices and financial reports sporadically, set a specific day of the week or month for these tasks. Tools like **QuickBooks** and **FreshBooks** can help automate parts of this process, making it even more efficient.

Example:

A small web design agency scheduled all their invoicing tasks for the last Friday of each month. By batching this process, they eliminated billing errors and improved cash flow management.

Using Templates and Checklists

Templates and checklists are invaluable for saving time on repetitive tasks and ensuring consistency. Whether you're drafting emails, creating project proposals, or onboarding new clients, having a template or checklist can streamline your workflow and reduce the chances of missing important steps.

Benefits of Templates and Checklists

- **Time Savings**: Templates eliminate the need to start from scratch every time, speeding up task completion.

- **Consistency**: Using templates ensures that all your documents have a professional and consistent format.

- **Reduced Errors**: Checklists help you stay organized and prevent mistakes, especially for complex tasks.

Examples of Using Templates and Checklists

1. **Email   Templates**
   If you frequently send similar emails—like follow-ups, client onboarding messages, or proposals—create templates for these emails. This allows you to quickly customize and send them, saving valuable time.

Example:
A real estate agent used to spend a lot of time drafting personalized follow-up emails after each property showing. By creating a set of email templates for different scenarios, she reduced her email drafting time by 50%.

2. **Project Management Checklists**
   Use checklists in your project management tools like **Asana** or **Trello** to ensure that all project tasks are completed systematically.

Example:

A software development firm created a project checklist template for each new client project, detailing all the necessary steps from initial consultation to final delivery. This checklist streamlined their workflow and reduced project completion times by 20%.

3. **Onboarding Templates**
   Creating an onboarding template for new employees or clients can help you get them up to speed quickly.

Example:

A boutique marketing agency developed an onboarding checklist for new clients, covering all necessary documentation, initial meetings, and campaign kickoff steps. This not only improved client satisfaction but also accelerated project initiation.

The Two-Minute Rule

The Two-Minute Rule, popularized by productivity expert David Allen in his book *Getting Things Done*, is a simple yet effective strategy for managing small tasks. The rule is straightforward: if a task will take two minutes or less to complete, do it immediately.

Why the Two-Minute Rule Works

- **Reduces Task Backlog**: Small tasks can accumulate quickly, leading to overwhelm. By handling them immediately, you prevent a backlog.

- **Boosts Momentum**: Completing quick tasks can give you a sense of accomplishment and momentum, making it easier to tackle larger projects.

Examples of the Two-Minute Rule in Action

1. **Responding to Quick Emails**
   If an email requires a brief response, reply to it immediately rather than leaving it in your inbox to address later.

Example:
A graphic designer adopted the Two-Minute Rule for responding to quick client inquiries, reducing

her email backlog and improving client communication.

2. **Tidying Up Your Workspace**
   Taking two minutes at the end of each day to organize your desk can improve your productivity the next morning.

Example:
An accountant found that spending two minutes each evening to organize paperwork and clear her desk helped her start the next day with a clear focus.

3. **Updating Task Lists**
   If you think of a new task, add it to your task management system like **Todoist** or **Microsoft To Do** immediately, rather than waiting and potentially forgetting about it.

Mindfulness and Breaks

In a world that glorifies busyness, it's easy to overlook the importance of mental health and taking breaks. However, working non-stop can lead to burnout, decreased productivity, and even health issues. Incorporating mindfulness and regular breaks into your daily routine can significantly improve your focus, creativity, and overall productivity.

The Benefits of Mindfulness and Taking Breaks

- **Reduced Stress**: Mindfulness practices like meditation and deep breathing exercises can help reduce stress levels, leading to better decision-making.

- **Increased Focus**: Short breaks, especially those that involve physical activity or a change of scenery, can refresh your mind and increase your focus when you return to work.

- **Boosted Creativity**: Stepping away from your desk allows your mind to wander, which can lead to creative breakthroughs.

Examples of Mindfulness and Break Techniques

1. **The Pomodoro Technique** This time management method involves working in focused 25-minute intervals (called Pomodoros), followed by a 5-minute break. After completing four Pomodoros, take a longer break of 15-30 minutes.

Example:

A freelance writer struggled with procrastination and staying focused. By adopting the Pomodoro Technique, she improved her writing efficiency and reduced burnout.

2. **Mindful** **Meditation**
   Practicing mindfulness meditation, even for just a few minutes a day, can help clear your mind and improve focus. Apps like **Headspace** and **Calm** offer guided meditations tailored for busy professionals.

Example:

The owner of a small graphic design studio started a daily 10-minute meditation practice using the Calm app, which helped her reduce stress and boost creativity.

3. **Physical** **Breaks**
   Taking short physical breaks, like a quick walk or stretching session, can reinvigorate your energy levels.

Example:

A small accounting firm encouraged its team to take a 5-minute stretching break every hour. This simple change improved employee morale and productivity.

Conclusion

Implementing productivity hacks like batch processing, using templates and checklists, adopting the Two-Minute Rule, and incorporating mindfulness practices can significantly improve your efficiency as a small business owner. These strategies are not just about working harder; they're about working smarter, making the most of your time and resources to drive business success.

Remember, the key to productivity is consistency. Start by integrating one or two of these hacks into your daily routine, assess their impact, and gradually build on them as you see fit. By continuously refining your productivity strategies, you'll create a more streamlined, efficient, and successful business operation.

In the next chapter, we will explore how **data analytics and performance tracking** can provide valuable insights into your business's performance, helping you make informed decisions and drive growth. Get ready to unlock the power of data to transform your business!

Chapter 7: Building a Productive Team Culture

As a small business owner, your team plays a pivotal role in your company's success. Building a culture of productivity not only improves your business's overall performance but also boosts morale, job satisfaction, and long-term employee retention. In this chapter, we will explore essential strategies for cultivating a productive team culture, from setting clear goals to fostering continuous learning and maintaining a positive work environment. These strategies will not only increase the efficiency of your team but will also contribute to the overall success of your business.

Setting Clear Goals and Expectations

One of the cornerstones of a productive team culture is the ability to set clear goals and expectations. When employees understand their roles, objectives, and how their work aligns with the company's broader vision, they are more focused, engaged, and motivated. Clear goals also provide a sense of direction, which is vital for both individual and team performance.

Why Clear Goals Matter

1. **Increased Focus and Motivation**: Employees who understand what is expected of them are more likely to stay focused and motivated. They have a clear roadmap that guides their actions and helps them prioritize tasks effectively.

2. **Performance Measurement**: Clear goals provide a benchmark for measuring success. Whether it's hitting sales targets, completing a project, or improving customer satisfaction, measurable goals allow you to track progress and identify areas for improvement.

3. **Alignment with Company Vision**: When individual goals align with the company's broader mission, it fosters a sense of purpose. Employees will feel like they are contributing to something bigger than themselves, which can increase job satisfaction and loyalty.

Examples of Setting Clear Goals

1. **SMART   Goals**
   The **SMART** framework (Specific, Measurable, Achievable, Relevant, and Time-bound) is a powerful tool for setting clear and actionable goals. For example, rather than a vague goal like "improve sales," a SMART goal would be "Increase sales by 15% over the next quarter by targeting new customers and enhancing the current marketing strategy."

Example:
A small marketing agency set a SMART goal for their content team: "Produce 10 blog posts in the next month targeting high-conversion keywords to increase organic traffic by 20%." The clarity of this goal helped the team stay focused and track their progress.

2. **Team-Based   Goals**
   In addition to individual goals, setting team-based goals encourages collaboration and accountability. For instance, a small team may have the collective goal of improving customer satisfaction by reducing response times.

Example:

A customer service team in a retail business set the goal to reduce average response time to customer inquiries to under 2 hours. Regular check-ins and performance reviews helped them stay on track, leading to an increase in customer satisfaction ratings.

3. **OKRs (Objectives and Key Results)**
   OKRs are another framework that helps set clear goals by breaking down objectives into measurable key results. This method is particularly effective for aligning individual goals with organizational priorities.

Example:

A tech startup used OKRs to align their product development team's goals with their broader business strategy. For instance, their objective was "Launch a new feature by the end of the quarter," and the key results were "Complete beta testing by week 6" and "Achieve a 90% satisfaction rate in the user survey."

Employee Productivity Tools

In today's fast-paced work environment, leveraging productivity tools to track and enhance employee performance is essential. These tools help streamline processes, monitor progress, and ensure that employees stay on track with their tasks. By using the right productivity tools, small business owners can enhance team efficiency, maintain accountability, and gather insights to make data-driven decisions.

Time Tracking Tools

1. **Time   Doctor**
   Time Doctor is a powerful time-tracking tool that helps business owners monitor employee productivity. It provides real-time tracking, which allows team members to log the time spent on various tasks. It also offers insights into how much time is being spent on productive versus

unproductive activities, helping employees optimize their work habits.

Example:

A digital marketing firm used **Time Doctor** to track the productivity of their remote employees. By reviewing the reports, they discovered that one of their team members was spending excessive time on meetings. After discussing the issue, the team member was able to streamline their meeting times, freeing up more hours for deep work, which improved overall productivity.

2. **Toggl**

   Toggl is another popular time-tracking tool that provides detailed insights into where time is spent throughout the workday. Toggl also allows for easy integration with other project management tools, making it a seamless choice for tracking tasks and employee performance.

Example:

A graphic design agency implemented **Toggl** to track the time spent on different projects. The data helped the team understand which tasks were taking longer than expected, allowing them to adjust their workflows and estimate future projects more accurately.

3. **Basecamp for Task Management**
   In addition to time tracking, **Basecamp** is an excellent tool for task management and collaboration. It allows employees to stay organized by creating to-do lists, sharing files, and tracking progress on various projects.

Example:

A software development company adopted **Basecamp** to assign tasks and deadlines to their employees. The tool's simple, user-friendly interface allowed team members to stay aligned with their responsibilities, leading to faster project completion and improved team collaboration.

Benefits of Productivity Tools

- **Accountability**: Productivity tools help keep employees accountable by providing a clear overview of tasks, deadlines, and progress.

- **Data-Driven Insights**: These tools offer valuable data that can be analyzed to improve workflows and optimize team performance.

- **Remote Work Efficiency**: For remote teams, these tools are essential for maintaining productivity and collaboration across different locations and time zones.

Encouraging Continuous Learning

A key factor in maintaining a productive team culture is offering opportunities for continuous learning and professional growth. When employees feel that they are growing in their careers and acquiring new skills, they are more engaged, motivated, and loyal to the company. Encouraging continuous learning not only benefits the individual employee but also contributes to the overall success and innovation of the business.

Why Continuous Learning Matters

1. **Skill Development**: In a rapidly changing business environment, keeping up with the latest trends, tools, and technologies is crucial. Continuous learning ensures that employees remain competitive and capable of handling new challenges.

2. **Increased Employee Engagement**: Employees who feel that they are developing professionally are more likely to be engaged in their work. This engagement leads to higher job satisfaction and reduced turnover.

3. **Improved Performance**: Offering learning opportunities helps employees develop their skills, which in turn improves their job performance and the overall effectiveness of the team.

Examples of Encouraging Continuous Learning

1. **Online Learning Platforms** Platforms like **Udemy, LinkedIn Learning**, and **Coursera** offer courses on a wide range of subjects. Business owners can encourage employees to take courses that align with their career goals or the company's needs.

Example:
A small e-commerce company offered its customer service team access to an online course on improving customer communication skills. As a result, the team's interactions with

customers became more positive, and customer satisfaction scores increased.

2. **Mentorship   Programs**
   Pairing less experienced employees with mentors can provide valuable guidance and foster skill development. Mentorship programs allow employees to learn from one another, increasing collaboration and knowledge sharing.

Example:
A tech startup introduced a mentorship program where senior developers mentored junior developers. This initiative not only accelerated the learning process but also fostered a sense of community within the team.

3. **Conferences   and   Workshops**
   Sending employees to conferences and workshops is a great way to expose them to industry trends and new ideas. Additionally, these events can serve as networking opportunities, enhancing both individual and company growth.

Example:
A digital marketing agency sent its entire team to an annual industry conference. The knowledge

gained from the event helped the team implement more effective marketing strategies, leading to a 25% increase in client acquisition.

Fostering a Positive Work Environment

A positive work environment is essential for fostering productivity, creativity, and collaboration. When employees feel valued, supported, and respected, they are more likely to put forth their best effort. Creating a positive work culture is about more than just offering a competitive salary—it's about building an environment that promotes well-being, teamwork, and job satisfaction.

Why a Positive Work Environment Matters

1. **Boosted Morale**: When employees feel supported and appreciated, they are more motivated to work hard and contribute to the team's success.

2. **Improved Retention**: A positive work environment leads to higher employee satisfaction, which reduces turnover rates. Employees are more likely to stay

with a company where they feel valued and supported.

3. **Increased Collaboration:** When employees feel comfortable in their work environment, they are more likely to collaborate and share ideas, leading to greater innovation and problem-solving.

Examples of Fostering a Positive Work Environment

1. **Recognition and Rewards** Recognizing employees for their hard work can go a long way in boosting morale. This recognition can take the form of praise, bonuses, or non-monetary rewards like extra time off.

Example:
A small consulting firm introduced an "Employee of the Month" program where the winner received a gift card and public recognition at a team meeting. This simple initiative led to increased motivation and a stronger sense of camaraderie.

2. **Team-Building Activities** Regular team-building activities, both in and out of the office, help strengthen

relationships and improve collaboration. Whether it's a monthly lunch, a team outing, or a problem-solving workshop, these activities foster a sense of community.

Example:

A design agency organized quarterly team-building outings, such as hiking trips or cooking classes. These activities helped employees bond and improved their ability to work together effectively on projects.

3. **Work-Life Balance**

Encouraging work-life balance is crucial for preventing burnout and maintaining long-term productivity. Offering flexible working hours, remote work options, and generous vacation policies can help employees feel more balanced and motivated.

Example:

A marketing agency introduced flexible work hours and allowed employees to work remotely twice a week. This policy contributed to improved employee satisfaction and reduced stress levels.

Conclusion

Building a productive team culture requires intention, effort, and a commitment to creating an environment where employees can thrive. By setting clear goals, leveraging productivity tools, encouraging continuous learning, and fostering a positive work environment, small business owners can create a team that is engaged, motivated, and highly effective. Investing in your team's success not only enhances business performance but also cultivates a workplace where everyone feels valued and supported. Through these efforts, you'll be well on your way to building a culture of productivity that drives your business forward.

Chapter 8: Measuring and Improving Productivity

In the fast-paced world of small business ownership, measuring productivity is vital to long-term success. As an owner, you need to understand how efficiently your business is operating, identify potential areas for improvement, and implement strategies to optimize performance. This chapter will explore how to measure and improve productivity through Key Performance Indicators (KPIs), regular performance reviews, continuous improvement strategies, and productivity tracking tools. By mastering these concepts, you can ensure that your business continues to grow and perform at its best.

Key Performance Indicators (KPIs)

Key Performance Indicators (KPIs) are essential metrics that help businesses track their progress toward specific objectives. By identifying and measuring KPIs, small business owners can evaluate their team's performance, identify strengths and weaknesses, and make data-driven decisions that foster growth and productivity.

Why KPIs Matter

KPIs provide a clear picture of how well a business is performing in different areas. Rather than relying on assumptions or guesswork, KPIs offer quantitative data that can guide decision-making and business strategies. Tracking the right KPIs also helps small business owners:

1. **Measure Progress**: KPIs provide a benchmark to track the business's progress toward its goals. For example, a goal of increasing sales by 20% over the

next quarter can be tracked using sales revenue KPIs.

2. **Identify Trends**: By tracking KPIs over time, you can identify patterns or trends, such as seasonal fluctuations in sales, that may influence business decisions.

3. **Ensure Alignment with Goals**: KPIs help ensure that all team members are working toward the same objectives. When each department or individual has specific KPIs tied to the business's overall goals, it becomes easier to measure individual contributions to the company's success.

Types of KPIs to Measure Productivity

1. **Sales Performance Metrics**
Sales are often the primary indicator of business success. Tracking KPIs such as sales revenue, sales conversion rates, average transaction value, and lead-to-customer ratio helps business owners understand how well their sales team is performing and identify areas for improvement.

Example:
A retail store may track monthly sales growth,

conversion rate (number of customers who make a purchase vs. those who enter the store), and customer acquisition cost (the amount spent on marketing to acquire a new customer). These metrics provide insight into the efficiency of the sales process and highlight opportunities for improving sales strategies.

2. **Customer Satisfaction Metrics**
   Metrics like Net Promoter Score (NPS), customer satisfaction surveys, and customer retention rates help measure how well the business is meeting customer expectations. Satisfied customers are more likely to repeat business and refer others, so focusing on customer-related KPIs is critical for sustained productivity.

Example:
A subscription-based service company regularly surveys its customers to measure satisfaction and gather feedback on areas for improvement. By tracking these scores over time, the company can identify trends and make necessary changes to improve customer retention.

3. **Employee Productivity Metrics**
   Measuring employee productivity is also

vital for improving business efficiency. Key metrics might include employee output (how much work is produced in a given time), task completion rates, or employee satisfaction scores.

Example:

A small accounting firm could track KPIs such as the number of tax returns completed per employee during tax season, the average time to complete a task, and client satisfaction scores. These metrics help the firm gauge employee productivity and determine where improvements might be needed.

4. **Operational Efficiency Metrics**
   Operational KPIs focus on streamlining processes, reducing waste, and improving efficiency. Examples of operational KPIs include production time, cost per unit of output, and inventory turnover rates.

Example:

A manufacturing business could track the number of units produced per hour, aiming to reduce production time while maintaining quality. By measuring these KPIs, the business can identify bottlenecks in the production process and implement improvements.

How to Choose the Right KPIs

Selecting the right KPIs depends on your specific business objectives. Consider the following when choosing KPIs:

- **Relevance**: KPIs should directly relate to your business goals. For example, if your goal is to increase revenue, then sales performance metrics are crucial.

- **Measurability**: Ensure the KPI is quantifiable. It should be easy to track and report on.

- **Actionability**: KPIs should help you make decisions. They should indicate areas for improvement and provide insights into the necessary actions.

Regular Performance Reviews

Performance reviews are an essential tool for small business owners to assess the progress of their employees and overall business operations. By conducting regular reviews, owners can provide feedback, set new objectives, and identify areas where employees and processes can improve.

Why Regular Performance Reviews Matter

1. **Clarifying Expectations**: Regular reviews allow business owners to discuss whether employees are meeting expectations, reinforce goals, and adjust as necessary.

2. **Fostering Accountability**: When employees know they will be evaluated regularly, they are more likely to stay focused and motivated. Performance reviews reinforce the importance of meeting goals and contribute to a culture of accountability.

3. **Providing Feedback for Improvement**: Reviews offer an opportunity to give constructive feedback to employees. When done correctly, feedback can inspire improvement and foster personal and professional growth.

4. **Identifying Training Needs**: Reviews can also highlight areas where employees may need additional training or resources. By addressing skills gaps, small business owners can ensure that their team continues to improve and grow.

How to Conduct an Effective Performance Review

1. **Set Clear Objectives**
   Before conducting a performance review, set clear objectives for the meeting. Review the employee's performance against specific KPIs, achievements, and goals. Be prepared to provide examples of both strengths and areas for improvement.

Example:
A small software development company has a quarterly review system where each employee's performance is assessed based on project completion, bug resolution rates, and teamwork. This gives both the employee and manager a clear view of where they stand and what needs to improve.

2. **Use a Balanced Approach**
   During the review, use a balanced approach by acknowledging accomplishments and addressing areas where the employee can improve. Constructive feedback is essential for growth, but employees should also feel recognized for their contributions.

Example:

A marketing manager receives positive feedback for successfully running a campaign but is also encouraged to improve time management when delivering reports. Offering both praise and constructive criticism helps maintain morale and motivation.

3. **Set New Goals**

   After reviewing performance, set new objectives for the employee to focus on. These goals should be realistic, measurable, and tied to the overall business strategy. This will give the employee clear direction and keep them engaged in the process.

Example:

After a performance review, a customer service employee is given a new target of reducing average response time to customers by 10% over the next quarter. This goal is specific, measurable, and directly linked to improving customer satisfaction.

4. **Follow-Up and Monitor Progress**

   Follow up on the goals and feedback discussed during the review. Regular check-ins can help employees stay on track and address any challenges they may face in meeting their objectives.

Continuous Improvement Strategies

Continuous improvement is a philosophy that focuses on the constant optimization of processes to improve quality, reduce waste, and increase productivity. There are several methodologies that small business owners can implement to achieve continuous improvement, with Kaizen and Lean being two of the most effective.

Kaizen Methodology

The **Kaizen** philosophy focuses on making small, incremental improvements over time. The idea is that by continuously improving, businesses can achieve significant long-term gains in productivity and efficiency. In a Kaizen culture, employees at all levels are encouraged to contribute ideas and suggestions for improving processes.

1. **Employee Involvement**: In a Kaizen-driven organization, everyone from top-level management to entry-level

employees is encouraged to contribute ideas for improvement.

2. **Small, Incremental Changes**: Instead of large, disruptive changes, Kaizen focuses on making small, manageable improvements that accumulate over time.

3. **Focus on Process**: The focus is on improving processes, not just individual performance. By optimizing the workflows and eliminating bottlenecks, businesses can achieve greater productivity.

Example:

A small restaurant implements Kaizen by encouraging waitstaff to suggest ways to improve service efficiency. One employee proposes a new seating arrangement to speed up customer flow, while another suggests a revised ordering system. These small changes lead to a noticeable improvement in wait times and customer satisfaction.

Lean Methodology

Lean focuses on minimizing waste and maximizing value. By optimizing processes and removing unnecessary steps, Lean methodologies help businesses operate more efficiently.

1. **Eliminate Waste**: Waste can come in many forms—time, materials, labor, or inventory. Lean focuses on identifying and removing these inefficiencies.

2. **Optimize Flow**: Lean emphasizes streamlining processes and improving the flow of work. This could involve simplifying workflows or eliminating unnecessary steps.

3. **Empower Employees**: Lean also encourages employees to take ownership of the improvement process. As with Kaizen, Lean encourages continuous input and collaboration from everyone in the organization.

Example:
A small manufacturing business implements Lean principles to improve its production line. By removing unnecessary steps in the assembly process and reducing inventory storage, the company is able to increase production while cutting costs and reducing downtime.

Tools for Tracking Productivity

To track and improve productivity, small business owners need tools that provide real-time data, insights, and performance metrics. Using analytics tools like **RescueTime** and **Clockify** can help monitor employee performance, identify bottlenecks, and optimize workflows.

RescueTime

RescueTime is a time-tracking tool that helps users monitor how much time is spent on various activities throughout the workday. By tracking time on applications and websites, RescueTime provides detailed reports about where time is being spent, helping business owners identify areas for improvement.

- **Focus on Time Management**: RescueTime helps business owners and employees understand where time is wasted, allowing them to make adjustments to improve efficiency.

- **Automatic Tracking**: Unlike traditional time tracking, RescueTime runs in the background and automatically tracks activities, making it less intrusive and more accurate.

Example:

A freelance graphic designer uses RescueTime to track time spent on client work, administrative tasks, and social media. After reviewing the data, they notice that they spend more time on social media than expected. The designer decides to limit social media time during work hours, improving overall productivity.

Clockify

Clockify is a time tracking tool that provides detailed reports on how employees spend their time. This tool helps business owners monitor employee performance, track billable hours, and identify inefficiencies.

- **Track Time Across Projects**: Clockify allows users to track time spent on specific tasks or projects, making it ideal for project-based businesses.

- **Generate Reports**: Clockify generates reports that can be used to assess productivity trends and make informed decisions.

Example:

A consulting firm uses Clockify to track time spent on client projects. By analyzing the data, they identify that certain clients require more time than initially anticipated. They use this information to optimize their scheduling process, ensuring more efficient use of their time.

Conclusion

Measuring and improving productivity is an ongoing process that requires a combination of tracking performance, providing feedback, and implementing continuous improvement strategies. By using KPIs, conducting regular performance reviews, embracing Kaizen and Lean methodologies, and utilizing productivity tracking tools, small business owners can create a culture of continuous improvement. This not only increases efficiency but also fosters a work environment where employees are empowered to contribute to the company's success.

Conclusion: Mastering Productivity for Small Business Success

In the world of small business, productivity is not just about getting things done—it's about getting the right things done efficiently and effectively. Productivity directly impacts a business's bottom line, customer satisfaction, and employee morale. However, increasing productivity is not a one-size-fits-all approach. It requires a combination of tools, techniques, and strategies tailored to each business's unique needs. In this conclusion, we'll recap the key takeaways from this guide, offer actionable next steps for integrating productivity strategies into your small business, and provide final thoughts to encourage a mindset of continuous improvement for long-term success.

Recap of Key Takeaways

Throughout this guide, we've explored various aspects of productivity that can help small business owners maximize efficiency, improve performance, and sustain growth. Here's a recap of the essential tools, techniques, and strategies discussed:

1. Time Management Strategies

We began by emphasizing the importance of effective time management in enhancing business productivity. Time is a finite resource, and mastering how it is allocated can make or break a business. Some of the core time management strategies discussed include:

- **Batch Processing**: Grouping similar tasks together to reduce the time spent switching between different types of work. This minimizes context-switching and improves focus.

- **Using Templates and Checklists**: Implementing pre-made templates and checklists to streamline repetitive tasks. By eliminating the need to start from scratch every time, you save valuable time and ensure consistency in your work.

- **The Two-Minute Rule**: Handling small tasks immediately if they can be completed in two minutes or less. This rule is incredibly effective in preventing procrastination and ensuring that nothing falls through the cracks.

- **Mindfulness and Breaks**: Recognizing the importance of mental well-being in maintaining high productivity. Taking breaks and practicing mindfulness can help you recharge, improve focus, and enhance overall performance.

2. Building a Productive Team Culture

Creating a productive work culture is a crucial element of achieving business success. An engaged, motivated team is more likely to perform at a higher level. Key strategies for building a productive team culture include:

- **Setting Clear Goals and Expectations**: Clear communication is the cornerstone of a productive team. When employees know what is expected of them, they are more focused and aligned with the company's objectives.

- **Employee Productivity Tools**: Tools like Time Doctor and Toggl help track employee performance, provide insights into how time is spent, and identify areas for improvement.

- **Encouraging Continuous Learning**: By offering training programs, workshops, and skill development opportunities, you can foster an environment where employees are empowered to grow.

- **Fostering a Positive Work Environment**: A positive work environment where employees feel valued and supported can significantly boost morale, increase job satisfaction, and lead to greater productivity.

3. Measuring and Improving Productivity

Effective measurement of productivity is key to making informed decisions and optimizing business processes. We discussed the importance of:

- **Key Performance Indicators (KPIs)**: By setting and tracking the right KPIs, business owners can evaluate performance in areas like sales, customer satisfaction, and employee productivity. These metrics guide decision-making and identify areas for improvement.

- **Regular Performance Reviews**: Consistent evaluations provide opportunities for feedback, recognition, and goal-setting. Performance reviews also help identify skill gaps and align individual contributions with the company's broader goals.

- **Continuous Improvement Strategies**: Implementing methodologies like Kaizen and Lean helps to continuously streamline processes, eliminate waste, and improve efficiency. These strategies foster a culture of constant growth and optimization.

- **Tools for Tracking Productivity**: Tools such as RescueTime and Clockify help track employee and team performance. These tools provide insights into how time is spent and identify opportunities for improvement.

Next Steps for Implementation

Now that we've covered the core strategies and tools for boosting productivity, it's time to turn this knowledge into action. Here are some concrete steps to help you integrate these strategies into your small business:

1. Prioritize and Identify Areas for Improvement

The first step to improving productivity is identifying which areas of your business need the most attention. This requires an honest evaluation of your current processes, tools, and performance. You might want to ask yourself:

- Where are bottlenecks occurring?

- Which tasks or projects take the most time and energy?

- Are there areas where employees are disengaged or underperforming?

By pinpointing the specific pain points, you can then choose which productivity strategies will have the most impact.

2. Implement Time Management Techniques

Start by introducing time management strategies to your team. For example, encourage the use of **batch processing** for tasks that can be grouped together (e.g., responding to emails or making phone calls). You can also implement **checklists** and **templates** for repetitive tasks to reduce the time spent on manual work.

For example, if you are a digital marketing agency, you could create templates for social media posts, ad campaigns, and client reports. This allows employees to work faster and more efficiently, ensuring that the business can handle a higher volume of work without sacrificing quality.

3. Integrate Employee Productivity Tools

Investing in tools like **Time Doctor**, **Toggl**, or **Clockify** can be incredibly beneficial in tracking employee productivity. These tools provide data on how time is spent across different tasks and projects, helping identify areas where time is being wasted or where employees may need more support.

- Start by introducing the tool to your team and provide adequate training to ensure everyone knows how to use it effectively.

- Set up time tracking for specific projects or departments, allowing you to monitor performance and identify opportunities for process optimization.

4. Set Clear Goals and KPIs

Start establishing KPIs that align with your business goals. For instance, if your primary objective is to increase sales, track metrics like conversion rates, lead generation, and sales growth. On the other hand, if you want to improve customer satisfaction, you might measure NPS (Net Promoter Score), response time, and customer feedback.

- Clearly communicate these KPIs to your team so that everyone understands what they're working toward.

- Track these KPIs regularly and adjust your strategy as needed to ensure that the business remains on course.

5. Foster a Positive and Engaged Team Culture

A productive team culture is one where employees feel valued, supported, and motivated to do their best work. Start by:

- Setting **clear expectations** for team members and regularly checking in on progress.

- Offering opportunities for **continuous learning** and growth, such as training sessions, workshops, or access to online courses.

- Building a **positive work environment** by recognizing accomplishments and promoting teamwork.

Incorporate regular team-building activities and encourage open communication. Recognize achievements, no matter how small, to foster a sense of accomplishment and motivation.

6. Implement Continuous Improvement Practices

Encourage a mindset of continuous improvement within your organization. This can be achieved by adopting **Kaizen** or **Lean** practices, which emphasize incremental improvements. For instance:

- Encourage team members to suggest improvements to processes.

- Hold regular meetings where team members can discuss inefficiencies and brainstorm solutions.

- Use feedback to continually refine workflows and eliminate unnecessary steps.

Start small by choosing one area of your business to optimize, such as customer service or project management, and then expand your improvement efforts as you see success.

Final Thoughts

Productivity is not just a buzzword—it's the lifeblood of any small business. When you prioritize productivity, you create a more efficient, engaged, and profitable business. This requires not only utilizing the right tools and strategies but also fostering a culture of continuous growth and improvement.

As a small business owner, your leadership and commitment to productivity will set the tone for your entire organization. By setting clear goals, investing in the right tools, and consistently evaluating and improving performance, you can achieve long-term success. Remember, productivity is a journey, not a destination. As your business grows, so too should your efforts to streamline processes and enhance efficiency.

Embrace the strategies and tools discussed in this guide, and begin implementing them in your business today. Start small, stay consistent, and celebrate every improvement along the way. With the right mindset and a commitment to productivity, you'll be well on your way to achieving business success that lasts.

Appendix: Additional Resources for Productivity Mastery

As you continue your journey toward improving productivity in your small business, the following resources, templates, and worksheets will further support your efforts. Whether you're looking to dive deeper into productivity concepts, find practical tools, or clarify some of the terms used throughout this book, this appendix is here to guide you. Below, you'll find:

- **Recommended Resources** for further reading

- **Templates and Worksheets** to implement productivity strategies
- **Glossary of Terms** to understand key productivity-related concepts

---

Recommended Resources

To deepen your knowledge and refine your approach to productivity, we've compiled a list of books, courses, and tools that will further enhance your understanding and implementation of the strategies discussed in this book.

Books

1. **"Getting Things Done: The Art of Stress-Free Productivity" by David Allen**

   - This classic book introduces the GTD (Getting Things Done) methodology, a system for capturing, processing, and organizing tasks and ideas. It's ideal for small business owners looking to increase efficiency and reduce stress by decluttering their minds.

2. **"The 7 Habits of Highly Effective People" by Stephen R. Covey**

   o Covey's timeless principles focus on personal growth, leadership, and prioritizing what matters most. It's a great read for business owners and employees alike who want to align their actions with their long-term goals.

3. **"Atomic Habits: An Easy & Proven Way to Build Good Habits & Break Bad Ones" by James Clear**

   o A must-read for anyone interested in habit-building, "Atomic Habits" focuses on how small, incremental changes can lead to remarkable results over time. This book offers actionable steps to build effective habits that can streamline your business operations.

4. **"The Lean Startup" by Eric Ries**

   o For small business owners looking to optimize their workflow, this book focuses on a systematic approach to creating and managing successful startups. It introduces Lean principles that can help entrepreneurs maximize efficiency and minimize waste in their operations.

5. **"Essentialism: The Disciplined Pursuit of Less" by Greg McKeown**

   o This book emphasizes the importance of focusing on the most important tasks, eliminating distractions, and doing less to achieve more. It's particularly useful for small business owners who feel overwhelmed with their to-do lists.

Courses

1. **"Time Management Fundamentals" on LinkedIn Learning**

   o This course offers a deep dive into essential time management techniques, including prioritization, planning, and delegation. It's a great resource for learning to structure your day more effectively.

2. **"The Complete Productivity Course" on Udemy**

   - A comprehensive course that covers everything from time management to workflow automation, this course is perfect for small business owners who want to improve efficiency in every aspect of their business.

3. **"Productivity Masterclass: Create a Custom System that Works" on Skillshare**

   - This course teaches you how to design your own productivity system, tailored to your unique needs. Whether you're looking to optimize personal or business productivity, this class offers actionable strategies to help you succeed.

4. **"The Power of Focus" on Coursera**

   - Designed for entrepreneurs and business owners, this course teaches you how to stay focused on key business priorities. Learn how to overcome distractions, maintain clarity, and increase your work efficiency.

Tools

1. **Trello** (https://www.trello.com)

   o A visual project management tool that helps teams collaborate on tasks. It's perfect for managing projects, setting deadlines, and tracking progress. With its flexible, drag-and-drop interface, you can easily prioritize and manage your business's workload.

2. **Asana** (https://www.asana.com)

   o Asana is a comprehensive project and task management tool designed to keep teams on track. With task assignment features, detailed reporting, and the ability to create recurring tasks, Asana can help streamline your business operations.

3. **Zapier** (https://www.zapier.com)

   o Zapier automates repetitive tasks by connecting apps and workflows. It's especially useful for automating routine administrative work, such as syncing data between software, sending follow-up emails, and posting on social media.

4. **RescueTime**
(https://www.rescuetime.com)

   o RescueTime helps you track how much time you spend on various applications and websites. It's useful for identifying productivity drains and optimizing work patterns by setting goals and alerts.

5. **HubSpot** **CRM**
(https://www.hubspot.com)

   o HubSpot CRM is an all-in-one tool for managing customer relationships, marketing campaigns, and sales. It's particularly useful for small businesses looking to integrate CRM functionality with automation to streamline customer communications and improve productivity.

Templates and Worksheets

To help you implement the strategies discussed in this guide, we've compiled a set of downloadable templates and worksheets designed to optimize your time management, streamline workflows, and track your productivity. These templates are easy to customize and will save you time while helping you stay organized.

1. Time Management Template: Daily Schedule

- This downloadable worksheet helps you structure your day using time blocks. It breaks down your day into focused intervals, ensuring you allocate enough time for high-priority tasks and allows for breaks to recharge.

[Download Time Management Template: Daily Schedule]

2. Task Prioritization Worksheet: Eisenhower Matrix

- Use this worksheet to apply the Eisenhower Matrix and categorize tasks based on urgency and importance. This tool will help you quickly assess what needs your attention and what can be delegated or delayed.

[Download Eisenhower Matrix Template]

3. Workflow Optimization Template: Standard Operating Procedures (SOPs)

- Standard Operating Procedures (SOPs) are crucial for maintaining consistency in your business operations. This template guides you through documenting repetitive tasks, standardizing processes, and training new team members efficiently.

[Download SOP Template]

4. Productivity Tracker: Weekly Overview

- This simple tracker helps you monitor your productivity each week. It allows you to set goals, track tasks completed, and review what worked or didn't. The goal is to identify patterns and areas where improvements can be made.

[Download Weekly Productivity Tracker]

5. Team Communication Checklist

- This checklist is designed to help you structure team meetings effectively. It includes sections for meeting objectives, discussion points, and action items, ensuring that team members are aligned and productive after every meeting.

[Download Team Communication Checklist]

Glossary of Terms

Understanding key productivity terms and concepts is vital for making the most of the strategies discussed throughout this guide. Below is a glossary of terms commonly used in the productivity world, which will help clarify concepts and provide more context for the tools and techniques mentioned in this book.

Key Productivity Terms

- **Time Blocking**: The practice of scheduling specific blocks of time for specific tasks or activities. This helps to eliminate distractions and ensures that important tasks are completed within a set time frame.

- **Batch Processing**: Grouping similar tasks together and completing them in one go, rather than switching between different types of work. This reduces time lost in transitioning between tasks and helps maintain focus.

- **Pomodoro Technique**: A time management technique where work is broken into intervals (usually 25 minutes), separated by short breaks. This method helps prevent burnout and improves focus by creating regular intervals for rest.

- **Standard Operating Procedures (SOPs)**: Detailed, documented instructions for completing tasks consistently and efficiently. SOPs ensure that processes are carried out the same way every time, reducing errors and streamlining workflows.

- **Key Performance Indicators (KPIs)**: Measurable values used to track the success of a business, project, or process. KPIs can include metrics like sales growth, customer satisfaction, and employee productivity.

- **Kaizen:** A continuous improvement methodology that focuses on small, incremental changes to improve efficiency and eliminate waste. It encourages all employees to contribute ideas for improvement.

- **Lean Methodology:** A business strategy that focuses on improving efficiency by eliminating waste, reducing costs, and enhancing productivity. Lean emphasizes continuous improvement and the involvement of all team members.

- **CRM (Customer Relationship Management):** A strategy and software tool used by businesses to manage interactions with customers and prospects. It helps businesses improve customer service, increase sales, and streamline marketing efforts.

- **Zapier:** A web-based automation tool that connects different apps and automates repetitive tasks by creating workflows known as "Zaps." Zapier helps businesses save time and reduce errors by automating tasks like data entry, notifications, and email marketing.

- **Time Doctor**: A productivity and time tracking software designed to track and analyze how employees spend their time. It provides insights into individual and team productivity, helping businesses improve work efficiency.

By utilizing these resources, tools, templates, and definitions, you can take meaningful steps to improve your productivity and enhance your small business operations. Whether you're just getting started or already implementing some of these strategies, the journey to increased productivity is one that will continually evolve. Stay committed to learning and adapting, and the benefits will soon be clear in the form of greater efficiency, reduced stress, and long-term business success.

Call to Action

Ready to Elevate Your Business with Expert HR Solutions?

At **Crystal Coast HR**, we specialize in providing comprehensive, tailored HR services designed to help your business thrive. Whether you need assistance with recruitment, employee relations, performance management, or compliance, our team is here to support you every step of the way.

Take the Next Step Today:

- Book a **free consultation** to discuss your unique HR needs.

- Explore our **services** and find the perfect solution for your business.

- **Contact us now** and start building a stronger, more efficient team with Crystal Coast HR.

Your business deserves expert HR support – let us help you grow and succeed! Reach out to Crystal Coast HR today!

David "Mike" Arnold | 252-668-1640

mike@crystalcoasthr.com